FlowerSong Press
McAllen, Texas 78501
Copyright © 2020 by Zamna Urista-Rojas

ISBN 978-1-73456194-4
Library of Congress Control Number: 2020946866

Published by FlowerSong Press
in the United States of America.
www.flowersongpress.com

Set in Adobe Garamond Pro

Typeset and design by Matthew Revert
www.matthewrevert.com

No part of this book may be reproduced without written permission from the publisher.

All inquiries and permission requests should be addressed to the Publisher.

A mi Jefito y Jefita, a mi Xelina, Tala, Suré y mi serrana . Y a todos/as ke plantan cara antes el miedo y la ignorancia, que encuentren el camino.

contents

9	One Again
10	Confined Bliss
11	Skips Through
12	Soft
13	Tortured Sky
14	Chanting
15	The Crack of Dawn
16	Can Awake
17	All In All
18	Always Near The Drain
19	Yo Bebo
20	No Child
21	R u
22	Eyes of Both Worlds
23	Yet Still Distant
24	The Window
25	Nourish
26	Wondering
27	Las Cortinas
28	The Noise
29	Demons
30	Amplified Souls
31	Howling
32	Reflection
33	Maybe There Should Be
34	Double-Fisted
35	Payed Attention
36	All That Remains
37	Distance
38	Eternal
39	Blooming Blood
40	Twitching
41	Temptress

42	Patience
43	Zancudos Que Cantan
44	Routine
45	Cockroaches Rising
46	I Sit Here
47	Invisible Chains
48	It's What's Pulling
49	Swallow
50	Concrete
51	Leave Me Residue
52	Seeds of Hope
53	Drunk Meditation
54	For You
55	Dizzy Resistance
56	Creatures
57	Calling Me Distance
58	Lengua de Disfraz
59	Design
60	Brothers of No Name
61	Ingenious Light
62	Living Theatres
63	Memorias de Metal
64	Quieta
65	Mordiscos de Alma
66	Gritando Infancia
67	Lejanos
68	Ni Veneno
69	Palacios
70	Waning Away
71	It's Way to Distraction
72	The Distance of Tradition
73	En Mis Brazos
74	Drying Your Wings
75	I Die at You
76	Huele a Tierra y Venganza

77	Sing, Curse
78	Through You
79	Dog Dances
80	Todavía
81	Go
82	Como Te Tengo
83	Tasks
84	That Was
85	Pared
86	A Través Del Viento
87	No Tiene Rostro
88	Conveniente
89	Ahora
90	Líneas
91	Quedará Flotando
92	Was King
93	Siempre
94	Viento
95	Un Día de Fuego
96	Mano a Mano
97	Claro y Intocable
98	Aunque Muriendo
99	Me Pierdo
100	Miedo de Tenerla
101	Afilado Sin Razón
102	Walking Through
103	So Loud
104	Flows
105	Sorry
106	Paralyzing
107	There Is No Point
108	Think
109	Between
110	Sevilla
111	Vine

All that remains
Eyes of both worlds
Cockroaches rising
In your presence
Leave me residue
calling me distance
lengua que disfrase
brothers of no name
I die at you
dog dances
drying your wings
the distance of tradition
blooming blood

One again

Dust holds an outline form
Turning high above
Scarred earth
Where
Somehow we've found solace here
We were brought here
By a new wind to consolidate
The future
While air trickles out our mouths
Like slow steam
Inside our massive shelter
Our perception
Our river has converged
Becomes one again
The world has stopped around us
I think to myself that's funny
Today the vultures are our
Guardians
Keeping a watchful eye from
their volcanic towers

CONFINED BLISS

I saw three times
Your reflection
On the wall
Through the reflection
And the recreation
Now realization liquefies
The recreation apart
Delusion is truth where
Solidity is not solid
But my circulation is…
It has been
Flowing in its confined
Bliss

SKIPS THROUGH

How does the boiling
Fill the water
Slowly devouring attention
A wave of direction
Who continues directing the reel?
As it skips through
Your memory

SOFT

The clouds are soft
As they pass by

TORTURED SKY

There was one who loved
Like a thin cloud
Pivoted on a split second of energy
Watching himself
Pass by over and over
In rectangle cages
His mother crying
"how long can you balance mijo?"
You can find us mumbling underneath
Looking for a way to unlock anything
A tortured sky

CHANTING

Blue
Planted firmly upside down
You are the horizon
Consistent rebirth
Your armada of awareness
Soon will be at your side
A million eyes waiting for their cue
The air suddenly slashed
All points in turmoil
Your flies can´t locate the pain
Because they are only messengers
Of passive interaction   soon
Will be chanting in darkness

The Crack of Dawn

The crack of dawn
Walking away from the spring
Melodies
Of asphalt
Of asphalt loved and loving
Fogs shadows
And despite the commotion
I lie in waiting
Watching
Absorbing
One step
One thousand tears
8000 birds
In my perpetual motion

can awake

Ambience high
The noise rising and falling
Like the ocean
Every once and awhile
Worlds are born through
Squared passages
Cold hunger emerges
Finally
Bravery
Begging delusion
For help
Shooed away
Before
The dreamer
Can awake
We
Might sleep
Indefinitely

all in all

One half stores energy
The other wastes
All in all
I am the duality
I long
To forget

always near the drain

Can you imagine
Never touching the floor
Always on
The second floor
Keep on sanding
Away
Downs pressuring
Me before
Incline does
Water smiling
Though uninvited
Smiling
As it forms
A puddle
Always near the drain
Metal trees
Singing under
A blue sky

YO BEBO

Yo bebo del
Sangre
Del viento acompañado
Por el humo
Enfrente
De plástico
Consoling
El calor
The winds bloody sweat

NO CHILD

My label...none
Where
When do I
Say your name
Still voices
Tension
No child
Was
No child is
Indirect exposure
Or
Mutated history

R u

R   u
Watt   zzz
I
  May
      Be
Wat
      Do
U   have fr me
Open arms
Wit
   Color
       Blind
  Eyes
   I
  Still
  The
  Eyes
  Still

eyes of both worlds

Half yours
Eyes of both worlds
Remember the present
Quickly if you can
It's sad though
What you've missed

YET STILL DISTANT

Blue light shooting out of
The corner of your eyes
Time to wish
Yet still distant
It's not light
Only lizards
On the dinner table smiling
And beg protesting
… Time to move on
Didn't you see the cat fly
By blood

THE WINDOW

Called braved
When
While
Muscles quiver under
My skin
Fish swimming by
The window of
Clear delusion
Who am I
When u r gone

NOURISH

The bats nourish
On my brittle bones
One thousand eyes
One thousand eyes
One thousand eyes

WONDERING

I can't seem to part the
Curtains
Light shining
Down
From behind your shadows
Wondering
Building tension
Just to learn to let go

Las cortinas

Las cortinas
Que no puedo
Partir
Y la luz callendo
Desde
Atrás
De tus
Sombras

THE NOISE

The noise talking
to me
so natural
without a self
there is no murder
chewing as we dine
rocks

Demons

Born with a drunk
Soul
Natural
Beauty
Smiles
Drunk… or not
Made
Make
ur own…
demons

amplified souls

Before death
I don't
Cut
My nails
Take my claws
Away from ur
Wretchedness
I am
Amplified
Souls
Let loose over
the city
buds
of indifference
staring at
ur etched existence

HOWLING

In darkness
Ur melodic
Howling
Continues
Hypnotic
Repetition
A clock of expression
Quieting the conditioned self

Reflection

To my reflection
I am not
A quick fix
The pill or
Another
Cell
Diseased tomorrow
It can't be…

maybe there should be

I see plumes
Or dark smoke
Where there is none
But maybe
There should be
Smudges,
Oceans of noise
And eyes
Crawling
Behind what it
Needs to be

DOUBLE-FISTED

There is noise…
On the river
Floating in plastic bags
"wanting," wanting
To swim, lurk
And carry you and your
Double-fisted
Flashes of confusion
Tiptoeing
Around spent
Matches
Frozen
Music
Blistered words

payed attention

Your skipping
Dripping into
sounds...
my air
waking
payed attention
whatever it wants
no games
gains
frames
shifting and kicking mirrors
down the street

all that remains

Shifting
All that remains
My reflected thumb
Arrested saliva
dropping impatiently
with the elevators
my breath secures itself
cubing the sky
the clouds
your energy smells of
youth
even time
likes to play
"all minds lean on crutches"

DISTANCE

Transporting my cubed awareness
The blur
Grows from my toes
It's all between my double
Hiding…
Lagartos…
In the corner of my eyes
Clumps of dust
Leaving full veins
Distance
Dissects
The present

eternal

They say you can hear my heart
When I hear none
Though its veins
Trickle out across
The damp air
To caress your hand
Our straight backs
Support
Bent skulls… as the
Festering bodies around us
Remain in denial
I intercept the sound
My blood rushing the sound
Of eternity

BLOOMING BLOOD

Simple grey
Determined pillars
Dancing
Against nails
Crooked crooked coughs
Against
Blooming blood

TWITCHING

Enjoy blue
Findings
Blankets upon
Irritation
Her square
Her circuses
Twitching as she speaks

Temptress

My state aura
Turning over and over
My chattering teeth
Shadows of nothing
Nowhere and no one
Spent energy
Hoping
Crooked dreams
Day to day
The real is unreal
Dancing in its purple
Curtains
True beauty
Curling her fingers around
Our spinal cord
I've lost what I had
… spectators
Hypnotized by the essence
Of the temptress
Curling her fingers around your spine

Patience

The patient mosquitos
To them I
Am not
This or that
Just limbs being
Torn off
The patient
Voices that echo
As the bell tolls

Zancudos que cantan

Zancudos que cantan
Llanto y gritos
De victory
Gritos de guerra
Y sus hermosos encantos

ROUTINE

Days i reinvent
Reinvented
Self and
Cats singing
Crooked looks
From my reflection
Only hers hurts
Cats screaming
Outside…
And the windows
Drunken geniuses scream
"el aire," el aire
Es la puerta
Suspendido
Inteligencia
So experienced and accustomed
To the routine
From destruction to life
And other
Twisted halls

COCKROACHES RISING

Full of smiles
So easy to forget
¨cultivate flowers¨
Whispers floating by
¨cultivate¨ echoing
Cockroaches rising
To the surface
… natures infinite
Brother laughing
Cause
They know who's gonna
win before the game
Starts
One thousand arms from
One body
Two minds

I sit here

I sit here
In one tone
Tones reverberating rivers
Of emotions
Where my ideas
Are just ideas
Nothing more
Just like me

Invisible chains

Attached to sight
Discrimination
Waits its
Turn
Patiently twiddling its thumbs
Darting eyes
Hope to exhaust the fear
Starting over
We excel in its repetition
Invisible chains
Invisible security
My body rotting on
The seashore as i
Sit there calmly
Watching

It's what's pulling

"not alien," Something calls
From within
My surroundings
Screaming but i hear little
"now," I see, colors
Simple etchings in the, air
I've never been lost
Just not listening
My surroundings
Understand
The message and
Feel the vibrations
You always do
It's what's pulling
At your innards, trying to rip it out
Why?
Because it's not dead yet

Swallow

Brace yourself
The light beginning to
leak in
as i swallow the darkness
my weapon
a blade of grass
against
a tear in your vision
and i´ve become weak
in your presence wondering
why we swallow
these crystal daggers

Concrete

Concrete
Altura
De su pesadísimo
Awareness… with it
coloring my senses
still playing with my shadow

Leave Me Residue

Leave me residue
Your bones…
Divinity
My hollow breaths
Here
only suffering
heals
staring through your injured reflections
I
   Love
        Your
                Silence
If that is what
You choose
Blades of ice
In my chest
Refusing to melt

Seeds of Hope

Who am i
You are
Beauty
Tiptoeing
In my embrace
Seeds of hope
Waiting to be nurtured

DRUNK MEDITATION

Devour
Drunk meditation
One month above the noise
Into the heavens
Limitless nothing
Distilled steps
On painted souls

FOR YOU

My heart racing
Through your suffering
Rage
The crevices
Ripping open
Bloody lubricated paths
Screaming
Sonic explosions
Inside my composure
For you…
Quietly
Crying

DIZZY RESISTANCE

Dying yesterday
Born, Suffering, Giving, Birth
Dualistic senses growing
Feeding out of ignorance´s palm
Today dying
Yesterday born
The sickness is
What makes you beautiful
Dizzy resistance and
Forgetting to breathe

CREATURES

Creatures
Socially drunk
The wilderness numb
My lips
My teeth
Impatiently sharp
Accustomed to my tilted head
And dog walks
The door slams
Dark staircases
Laughter from my childhood

Calling me Distance

The beast′s
  Heart
      Parts
The ones
     That don′t cry
Calling me distance
Calling me inconstant
   figures burning
      in our minds

Lengua de disfrace

Mi lengua organiza
Las penas
Los detalles
Lengua que disfrace
Mis emociones
Lengua de opciones
Y con mi acento
Te robo

Design

An ocean
Of translations
Boiling as
  I lock myself
In my room
    Hoping for heat
Going back to
Your treacherous
Home
        Full of technicians
      Designing
          Your consciousness

BROTHERS OF NO NAME

Ironic fusion
   After death
Who is gravity?
   Deceive me
With laughter
     Ridiculous
        Intentions
Drying hearts
   Lonely
      Surfaces my reckless
Brothers of no name
      Suffering
        They are kings,
Drunk solutions
      Drops of water
Smelling of
    exaggerated
harmony
   you can´t phase my disasters
and in my dreams, you are free

INGENIOUS LIGHT

Roses dancing in the shadows
 My deaf attention
Rushing to
Its next illusion
They're
 in the corners
under the cars
roses dancing
wherever
 ignorance's
 ingenious light
can't reach

LIVING THEATRES

Your disguised
   Lips innocence
Blistered
         Devoted time
Your living theatres
         Are ending

memorias de metal

Mira como bailan las nubes
Sus pisadas silenciosas
Y la frescura de su presencia
Acariciando la piel
   Instantes que no paran
      Y dulces besos
         En mis manos
Memorias de
    Metal
       De estructura
Y corazones

Quieta

A ti vengo
Sin mis ojos
Dulces sorpresas
Quieta la sangre
Sonriéndote de la oscuridad

MORDISCOS DE ALMA

Brillante los
Dientes
Que me esperan
   Y hambre que no quita
Mordiscos del alma
  Culpando
La tierra que cambia
Debajo de mis pies

GRITANDO INFANCIA

Esto era después
Que yo vi, la cara del
Agua estancada
Y ocupado creyendo
Cosas que no nos
Hace falta
Emociones que muerden
Que lloran
Gritando infancia
Afilaos son los momentos
Y esos son los bichos
Que nadan sobre
El superficie

LEJANOS

Lejanos respiros
Y las cosas
Que corren en
Mis venas
   Quemando
   Las cosas que
Los dioses de acero
        No roban

ni veneno

No hay cura
Que me abrace
Ni veneno que me mate
Y son las sombras
Cayendo encima
De la ciudad
Que siguen creciendo

Palacios

No hubo destinación
Curioso, la negra pared
Donde charla
   El enfermo y
El que no camina
Deja que se caigan
Construyendo sus palacios
   Debajo de la verdad

waning away

Natural, drunk, hiccups
Sweat, throats, venom
I hear the sounds
Waning away
Through the things i don´t
Do, poetry, visible, lust
Moments instants of delusions
Pleasure and unwanted images
Mandato que me mueve
Y tragando los detalles
I climb amongst my character

ITS WAY TO DISTRACTION

The rhythm slowly working
Its way to distraction
Capabilities no longer
Mine
   Artificial
Through my canine
Eyes…
Es que
Se llora, gritando
Desde mis manos
Niños esperados
  Que nunca vienen

The distance of tradition

An ocean
  You'll wash you out
Asking the asker…
  Mannequins
And gods of explanations
The distance of tradition
Beating its drums
  Your disasters and realizations
Watch how the reeds
  Dance to soft
  Music in the tide

en mis brazos

Who am i
When streets sing
La música suena
Y la perra llora
No hay autobuses pa' bajar
Ni torres que subir
Mido mi cuerpo en la pared
Y eternidad en mis brazos

Drying your wings

Where there is none
Needs and ideas evaporate
Drying your wings
Next to this mountain
Of inconsistency
Reactions that absorb the sun
Energy in our veins
Fluctuation composure
Moving into position
Until the next sessions

I die at you

I die at you
In rain´s lust for extremes
Wounds that don't exist
Blinking through
These slow erratic moments
Of despair and acidic juices
I can't cure
Though your blood
covers skies

Huele a tierra y venganza

I just wrote
This carnal rain
Back to the veins
Back to these elements
Pouring down through
My ideas
  And burning down
The apparitions
My dead skin
Blown away
Scales of memory
Carcasses de ayer
And our painful
Rebirth
Huele a tierra y venganza

SING, CURSE

Only 2 pages
Left in my caos
Ideas watching theirs
    Burn
And grinding teeth
Sing, curse
With my skin taken
away
I am no longer
Cold
When I drink
My memory
And its bitter
Love

THROUGH YOU

For you, tomorrow
Always exists
Having to live
Through you
Before I can
Live through me

Dog Dances

Let the
Dog dances
Rant and rave
Criminal nature
The games
Pasatiempos
Cuando me olvido
Cómo escuchar

todavía

Check the Sharp
Edges del charco
Porque, como es
Que llorando y cansado,
En la orilla
Los niños todavía
Tienen sed

Go

Time to go to work
The clock ticks
The door shuts
The dusts falling
The arms opening
The waters flowing
In my heart
Beating a new rhythm

como te tengo

My fingers
Together
Warm and
 Held
I am forgotten
 And
Missed
Como te tengo
Entrc cl alma
Y el cielo

Tasks

Who can die
And live
Where is choice
Who can suffer
Acceptance
And live
With death
The mentor
Acceptance
And its tasks

That Was

That was aggression, that's sharpening the baby's teeth
That was our shadow
   Under the bridges
That was their cardboard
   Community
That was hungry children
That was civilization
   Intelligence
      Guidance
That was dying alone
That was what we don't want
    To know
That was our capabilities
That was our great species, that was our infested planet
That was another
  Mother unappreciated
That was self-destruction, that was playing god
That was ignoring the truth, that was ignoring yourself
That was reckless desperation
That was a tragic loss, that was everyone's loss
That was life
That was not an excuse, that was ignorance
But not an excuse and this is now

PARED

Tu inestabilidad
Enfocando
Mañana
El desaparecido de voluntad
Amor
Lo invisible esperaba
Tropezando en tu riza
Prisiones de justicia
Paredes de hormigón
Y belleza
Lo que las luces
No me dejan ver

a través del viento

Que nunca podre tener
Llorare por el niño
Que me llama
a través del viento
y mal digo
los arcos que
Me condenan

no tiene rostro

Fluidity
Of lives
The growing pressure
Who fights
The metal hulls
Of your sinking ship
No tiene rostro

conveniente

Y empezando a discriminar
Enfermo
Escondido
Todas nuestras células
Conveniente
Mundos
En el umbral
De tu segregación

ahora

Mañana
Estoy condenando a despertar
Cuando me daré cuenta
Ahora…
Como podre vivir…
Atreves
Este ego atragante
Desapareciendo
En sus entrañas
Mi ego
Lo destruye

Líneas

Relojes olvidados
Líneas descuidadas
O lo que tu quieres llamarle
Escondido o protegido
Y las líneas entre
Riesgo
Una posibilidad
Juegos, rechazos
Y la entrada
De aturdimiento

QUEDARÁ FLOTANDO

Bailando con las sombras
Amargura y tiempo sigue
El aroma no se puede
Y antes nuestros ojos
… quedará flotando
Que nunca te llegara
Un amor profundo
La neblina te acaricia
Enamorado de tu rostro

was king

I was there
When they tore it
Down and inferiority was
King
The power of belief
Temporary salvation
And i'm told there's no
Time to refine
When take blood
To conserve blood
Is law

siempre

Trying to anticipate
I don't know
How i got here
Gotas de agua que, no se esparcen
Y el viento de Marruecos, llenando mi barriga
Está siempre al otro lado
Of this intentional wall
Reminding you not to look me in
The eyes

viento

Y entiendo nada
Sin direccion
Me paso de las oportunidades
Con el viento
La palma de la mano
La oscuridad, cielo
Alto y oscuro contra
Lo que fluye desde
Las entrañas
De los dientes

UN DIA DE FUEGO

Ahora
Que te salvara
Ni mi sonrisa
Yo no era
Pa' lagrimas
Ni tiempo
Y yo a ti te cuidaba
Un día de fuego

mano a mano

Aunque
llevandome nunca llegará
Hermano de miedo
Mano a mano
En eso que no consigue llegar
Tu elegancia llama
Y baja la tierra
Victimas
Que me entiendan
No hay

CLARO Y INTOCABLE

Porque no siento na
Y me duele
Van mano a mano
Borracheras y esperanza
Me quedo donde caigo
Y lugar
Ni siquiera tengo nombre
Claro y intocable
El cielo
Y putas follando
Madres llorando
De perdicíon
Días enteros

aunque muriendo

Soy la plataforma
Y bailando
Los niños
Pasa la energia
Encima de mi alma
Que sangrando
Como puede ser
Que aunque
Muriendo
Consegui mi
Forma

me pierdo

Me pierdo, me encuentro
Cuando pienso, me encuentro
Me pierdo, cuando pienso

miedo de tenerla

Y dulce acariciando mis ojos
Piel suave como el viento
Y yo la quiero
Los que la han visto
Tienen miedo de tenerla
Lloran por eso
Porque te conozco
Por tus maneras

afilado sin razón

Tu eres típico
Y muerto como
El terreno
Calvo, afilado sin razón

WALKING THROUGH

Reverberated
Your destructive
Footsteps
Walking through
These generations of
New faces, old plans

SO LOUD

My
Carcasses on my plate
And my silence
Is so loud
My heavy breaths
And the heavy sun
Timeless consciousness
And blinding colors
Giving me warmth

FLOWS

Even though
Outside the current
Flows
Inevident connections
And eminent reunions
Endless ideas
Endless ideas
Endless present
Endless camino
Endless consciousness and
Endless change
To be accepted

SORRY

And i miss took you
For your shadow
I´m sorry

Paralyzing

No disguise
No need
Piercing through me
Standing before me
Unconscious of his beauty
And its paralyzing warmth
Hope asks for little
And patience can only
Embrace one thing
Though
Asking for exactly what it wants

THERE IS NO POINT

There is no point
Of reference
In a world of image
No entrance
No exit
And my conscience
Is inconvenient

THINK

And they
Think
They have
Organized
Metal
Organized
Elements

Between

These are your hands
And the dew that
Trickles from your tongue
Subdues
Awareness
And embraces
The freedom floating
Between life and death

Sevilla

Sevilla de murciélagos
Y dátiles importados
Amores mas
verdes que el rio

vine

The patient vine
Constantly caresses
The river, forgetting
To think of her
Tired breath in
My lonely awareness

Zamna Urista-Rojas, born en Kalif Aztlan 1977. Childhood full of adventure and mudanzas, I remember music and colors. Las playas de Tijuana hasta los picos de los Rockies, and back again. El pan dulce que me compraba mi abuelita, las bandas de mis primos, the scary paintings of Frida en el salón. The garage full of books, treasures without limit that I slowly went discovering throughout the years. The psychedelic records de mi padre that my hermanito and I cherished, the murals of Xicano Park , what I thought was the most beautiful place on earth, as if walking in the presence of gods. Identity crisis, chaos, the ocean , el monte, the confusion. Waking up super early to go fishing en Avila, to barely catch anything over 6 hours and still feel like a king. Making our first fires alone and working on my puntería with the bow my Jefito made us. Throwing blows everywhere I could get away with it until I hit Junior high and realized I ain shit. These pendejos all decided to grow to the size of adults and I was lagging, still am. The long road to San Anton lined with roadkill. Catfish under the bridge, chuetes, pecan pralines and pecan trees at the old haunted family house. Cicadas singing to the sun, cottonmouth vipers in the tub, sitting by the bonfire scared shitless of my Tio's dark as night wolfdog. Late night runs for tacos al pastor, mi jefita pide "Contrabando y traición " al trio. The trailer homes, and Grandpa Lupe's yard full of unfinished cars. His glasses, his cap, beautiful red skin, fading tattoos, y como no, su lira. Working in Alaska in summer, wild times, wild animals and wild people. Mi padre cogiendo el armadillo y cantando como un guerrero. My collection of knives and cassettes of Bob Marley. Punk rock, Heavy Metal, Flamenco, Jazz , Cantautor. Tuning and then detuning, La guitarra me salvó el alma, pero luego el bolsillo también, didn't see that coming. In Andalucia of all places, nearly 10 years and now 10 more in Berlin. Sometimes when you don't know where to turn, you write. Your hidden voice, that hidden blade that opens your soul in front of a mirror. Años de busqueda and I know less everyday.

www.ingramcontent.com/pod-product-compliance
Lightning Source LLC
Chambersburg PA
CBHW052206090526
44583CB00017BA/2398